Collins

Revised Edition

Vision 5

A Course on Values and Life Skills

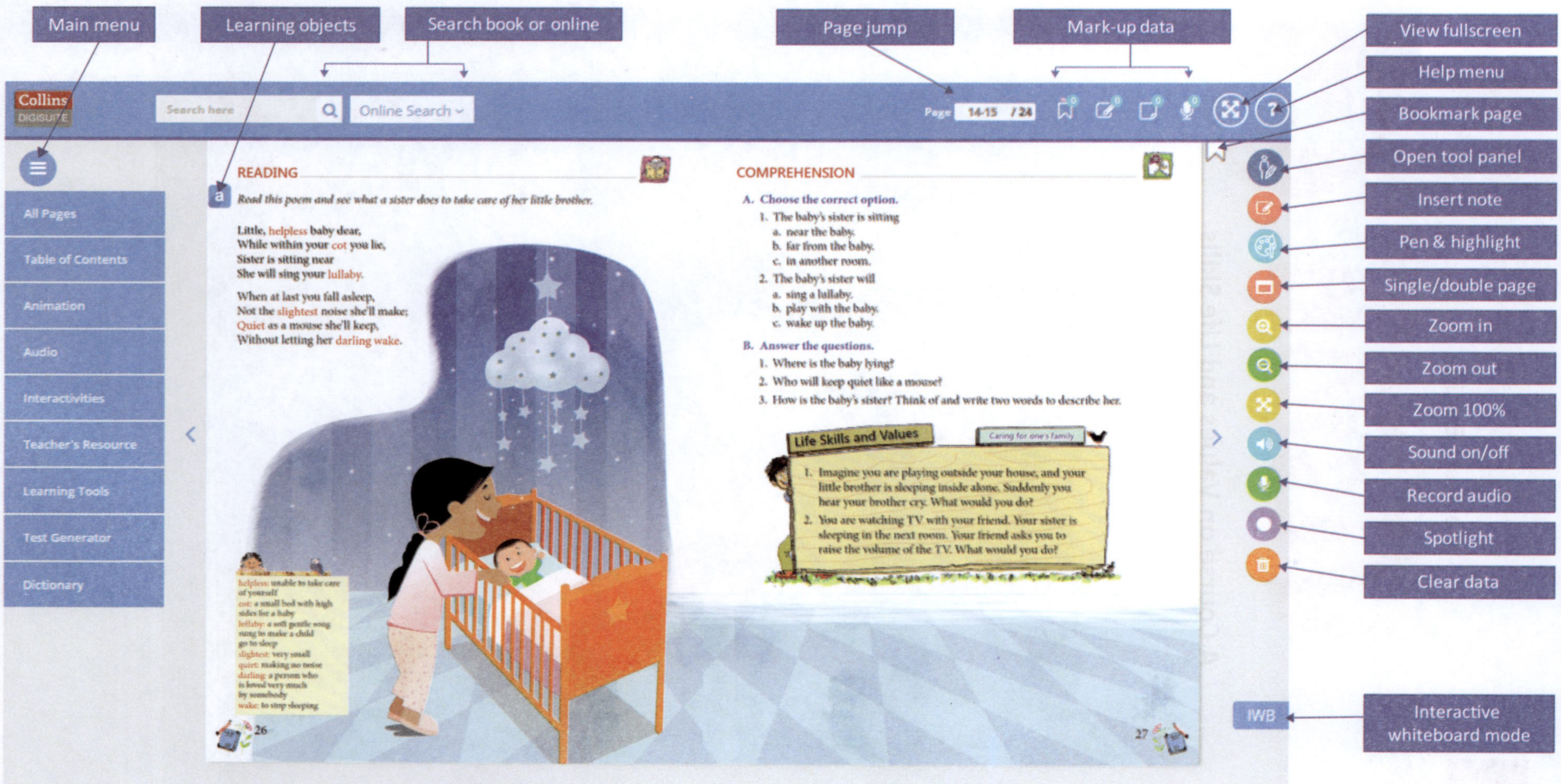
Main menu
Learning objects
Search book or online
Page jump
Mark-up data
View fullscreen
Help menu
Bookmark page
Open tool panel
Insert note
Pen & highlight
Single/double page
Zoom in
Zoom out
Zoom 100%
Sound on/off
Record audio
Spotlight
Clear data
Interactive whiteboard mode
Collins
DIGISUITE
Search here
Online Search
Page 14-15 / 24
All Pages
Table of Contents
Animation
Audio
Interactivities
Teacher's Resource
Learning Tools
Test Generator
Dictionary
IWB
READING
Read this poem and see what a sister does to take care of her little brother.
Little, helpless baby dear,
While within your cot you lie,
Sister is sitting near
She will sing your lullaby.
When at last you fall asleep,
Not the slightest noise she'll make;
Quiet as a mouse she'll keep,
Without letting her darling wake.
COMPREHENSION
A. Choose the correct option.
1. The baby's sister is sitting
a. near the baby.
b. far from the baby.
c. in another room.
2. The baby's sister will
a. sing a lullaby.
b. play with the baby.
c. wake up the baby.
B. Answer the questions.
1. Where is the baby lying?
2. Who will keep quiet like a mouse?
3. How is the baby's sister? Think of and write two words to describe her.
Life Skills and Values
Caring for one's family
1. Imagine you are playing outside your house, and your little brother is sleeping inside alone. Suddenly you hear your brother cry. What would you do?
2. You are watching TV with your friend. Your sister is sleeping in the next room. Your friend asks you to raise the volume of the TV. What would you do?
26
27

Preface

Vision **Revised Edition**, a course on life skills and values, is an engaging value education series meant to enable learners lead a balanced, happy and successful life. The National Education Policy, 2020 proposes the revision and revamping of all aspects of the education structure to create a new system that is aligned with the aspirational goals of 21st century education, while building upon India's traditions and value systems. It also lays focus on critical life skills and values.

Vision Revised Edition follows an interactive and multidisciplinary approach and caters to all kinds of learners with different learning styles.

Values are presented through progressively graded stories, anecdotes or poems.

Life Skills as laid down by the World Health Organization (WHO) have been covered through interesting stories.

Each book contains special chapters and colourful spreads showcasing the **United Nations Sustainable Development Goals**, which are important to achieve a just and an equitable world for all.

21st Century Skills have been mapped to each chapter with the aim of creating well-rounded individuals thriving in a constantly changing world.

Mental health and well-being of young learners is of prime importance in today's world. Therefore, **Let's Do Yoga** poster has been introduced as a brand-new feature of the book. It contains simple and doable asanas with step-by-step guidance and illustrations.

The series also focuses on mindfulness and social-emotional learning through **'happiness activities'**. Young children learn by doing, hence the series has a variety of hands-on activities, encouraging quiet reflection and sound action.

Creating a safety net for children and making them aware of **child rights** is much needed in this age and time. *Vision* Revised Edition has special advice for children through which they can face situations in which they feel afraid, pressurized or unsafe.

Vision Revised Edition comes with **Collins DigiSuite** which offers digital content packed with animated stories, slideshows and interactive activities.

***Vision* Teacher's Manuals** offer comprehensive **Lesson Plans** and **Additional Worksheets** for teachers.

In This Series ...

Vision Revised Edition adheres to the National Education Policy, 2020. Features such as 21st Century Skills, Life Skills, multiple intelligences, Sustainable Development Goals and Let's Do Yoga all align with the new policy.

Discuss

Warm-up exercise familiarizes students to the mood of the chapter

Read along

A story or a poem based on a value

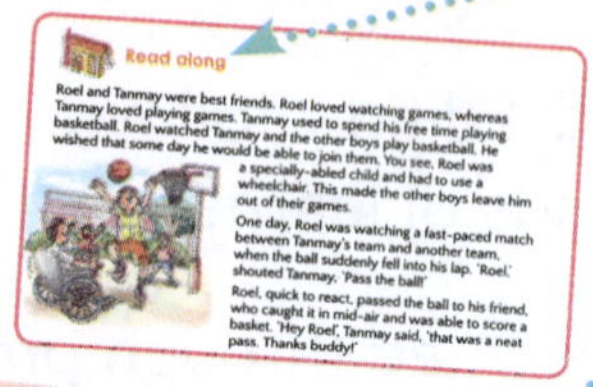
Read along

Roel and Tanmay were best friends. Roel loved watching games, whereas Tanmay loved playing games. Tanmay used to spend his free time playing basketball. Roel watched Tanmay and the other boys play basketball. He wished that some day he would be able to join them. You see, Roel was a specially-abled child and had to use a wheelchair. This made the other boys leave him out of their games.

One day, Roel was watching a fast-paced match between Tanmay's team and another team, when the ball suddenly fell into his lap. 'Roel,' shouted Tanmay. 'Pass the ball!'

Roel, quick to react, passed the ball to his friend, who caught it in mid-air and was able to score a basket. 'Hey Roel,' Tanmay said, 'that was a neat pass. Thanks buddy!'

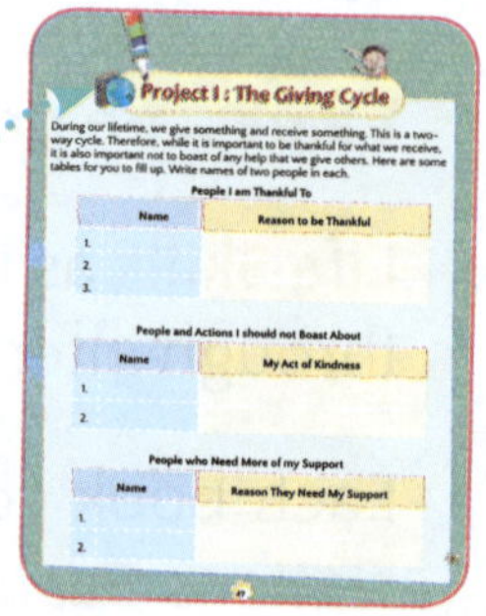
Project 1 : The Giving Cycle

People I am Thankful To

Name	Reason to be Thankful
1.	
2.	
3.	

People and Actions I should not Boast About

Name	My Act of Kindness
1.	
2.	

People who Need More of my Support

Name	Reason They Need My Support
1.	
2.	

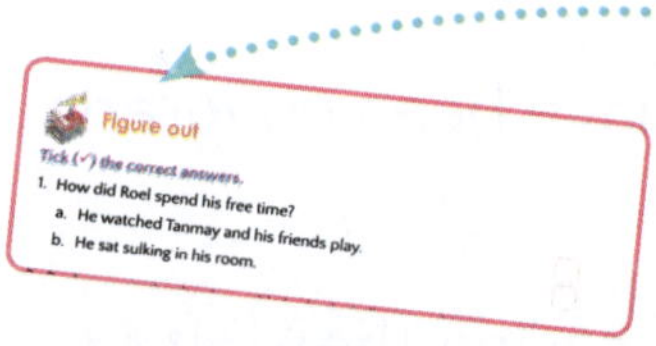
Figure out

Tick (✓) the correct answers.

1. How did Roel spend his free time?
   a. He watched Tanmay and his friends play.
   b. He sat sulking in his room.

Figure out

Questions based on the chapter to ensure value inculcation

Relate

Application-based questions to check students' understanding

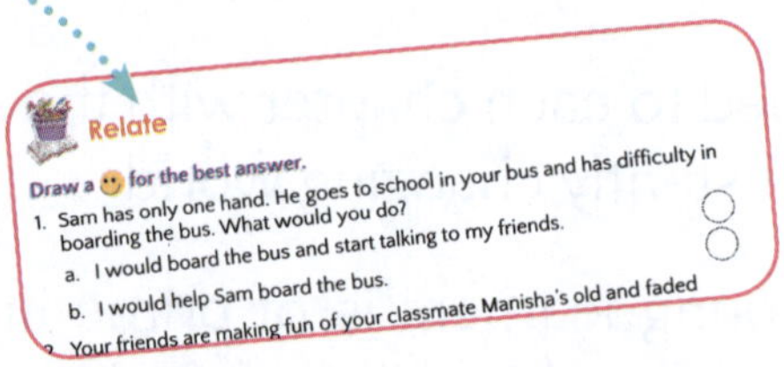
Relate

Draw a 🙂 for the best answer.

1. Sam has only one hand. He goes to school in your bus and has difficulty in boarding the bus. What would you do?
   a. I would board the bus and start talking to my friends.
   b. I would help Sam board the bus.
2. Your friends are making fun of your classmate Manisha's old and faded

Project

Interesting projects based on the values taught

Happiness Activity

Interesting activities to promote 'happiness'

Happiness Activity

Today, we use electronic devices such as laptops, mobile phones and tablets. While using them, we should know how to behave.

Tick the things that you should do while using mobile phones.

We should keep our phones on silent mode when we meet someone.

We should first ask the person we call if it is a good time to talk to them.

We should play on our mobile phones while in restaurants or in family functions.

We should talk softly on the phone when in a public place or while using public transport.

We should peep into other people's phone screens.

We should eat while using our phones.

Workout

Interesting worksheets that reinforce the value taught

Remember

Brief pointers that the students can incorporate in their behaviour

Think and Say

Thinking questions that encourage students to think laterally

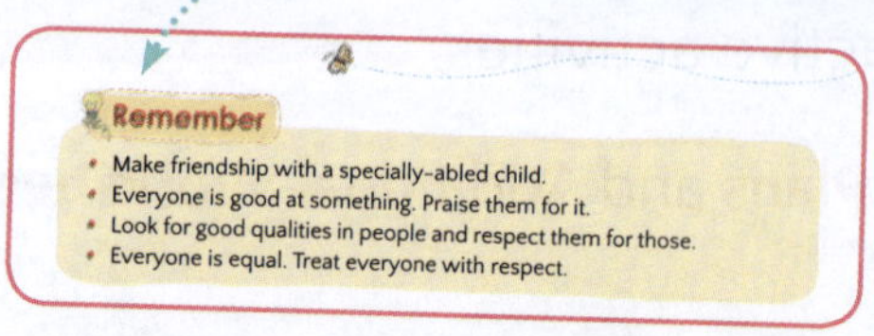
Remember

- Make friendship with a specially-abled child.
- Everyone is good at something. Praise them for it.
- Look for good qualities in people and respect them for those.
- Everyone is equal. Treat everyone with respect.

Think and Say

Your friend who cannot run very fast wants to play carrom and you want to play hide and seek. What would you do?

Happiness Box

Enjoyable activities that promote 'happiness' and exercises based on multiple intelligences addressing different learning styles

- Musical
- Interpersonal
- Visual-Spatial
- Verbal linguistic
- Naturalistic
- Intrapersonal
- Logical Mathematical
- Bodily Kinesthetic

Child Rights and Empowerment

Useful, child-centric advice to create a safety net for children and make them aware of their rights

Sustainable Development Goals

Special chapter and a colourful spread showcasing the UN Sustainable Development Goals, a set of goals aimed at changing our world for better

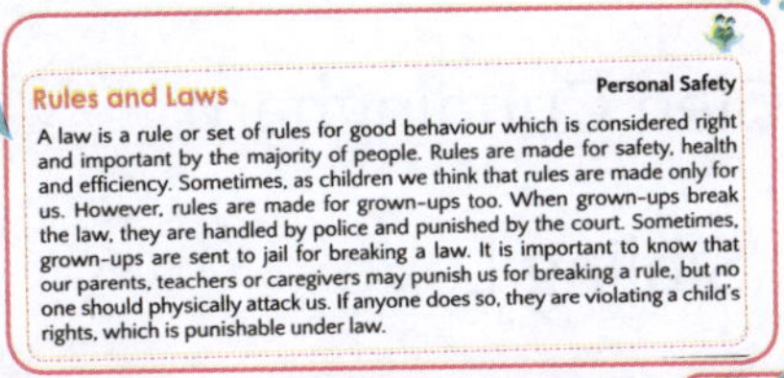

Rules and Laws — Personal Safety

A law is a rule or set of rules for good behaviour which is considered right and important by the majority of people. Rules are made for safety, health and efficiency. Sometimes, as children we think that rules are made only for us. However, rules are made for grown-ups too. When grown-ups break the law, they are handled by police and punished by the court. Sometimes, grown-ups are sent to jail for breaking a law. It is important to know that our parents, teachers or caregivers may punish us for breaking a rule, but no one should physically attack us. If anyone does so, they are violating a child's rights, which is punishable under law.

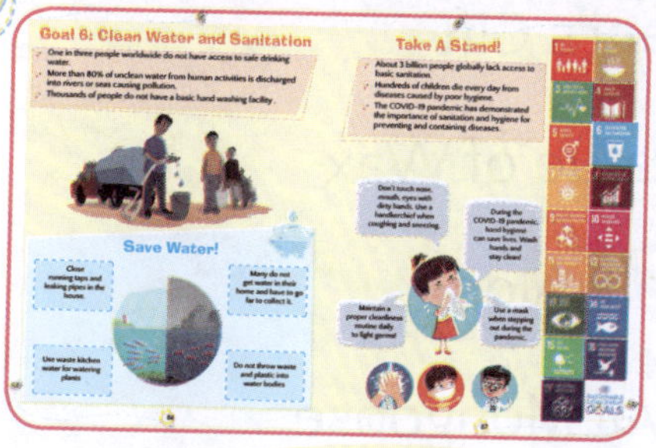

Poster

Colourful and interesting pull-out poster showcasing easy Yoga asanas

21st Century Skills

Skills necessary to succeed in the age of information: learning skills, literacy skills and social skills

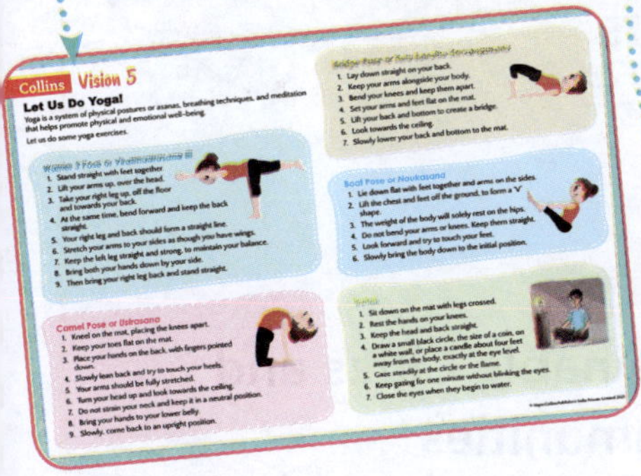

Life Skills

Chapters focusing on WHO life skills through interesting stories

Teaching tips

- Emphasize on honesty in actions.
- Talk about integrity and how important it is in all walks of life.
- Have a discussion on being honest to oneself.

Teaching tips

Suggestions for teachers

Detailed Contents

Values

Sustainable Development Goals

21st Century Skills

Learning Skills	Creative Thinking	The Statue of Wax
	Communication	Sibling Love
	Critical Thinking	Rani's Gift
Literacy Skills	Cultural and Civic Literacy	Walk Alone
Social Skills	Tolerance and Objectivity	Its Okay To Be Different
	Ethical Behaviour	Emperor Ping
	Leadership	The Best Prefect
	Creative Thinking	The Statue of Wax
	Initiative	The Loyal Mongoose

Life Skills

Happy Birthday, Grandmother Brave Akio	Interpersonal Relationship Coping with Stress

Projects

Project I Project II	The Giving Cycle Building Character Strength

Contents

1. Its Okay to Be Different

Discuss

Look at the pictures. Discuss them in class.

Read along

Roel and Tanmay were best friends. Roel loved watching games, whereas Tanmay loved playing games. Tanmay used to spend his free time playing basketball. Roel watched Tanmay and the other boys play basketball. He wished that some day he would be able to join them. You see, Roel was a specially-abled child and had to use a wheelchair. This made the other boys leave him out of their games.

One day, Roel was watching a fast-paced match between Tanmay's team and another team, when the ball suddenly fell into his lap. 'Roel,' shouted Tanmay, 'Pass the ball!'

Roel, quick to react, passed the ball to his friend, who caught it in mid-air and was able to score a basket. 'Hey Roel', Tanmay said, 'that was a neat pass. Thanks buddy!'

That night, Tanmay had an idea. He thought, 'If Roel could pass the ball so well without being trained, I wonder what he would be able to do after proper training and practice'.

The next day, Tanmay kept passing the ball to Roel, and his friend returned each pass accurately and successfully. This convinced Tanmay that Roel should be given an opportunity to play in a proper basketball match. His friends and coach had also seen the way Roel was quick to catch and pass the ball. After a long discussion, Tanmay, his coach and friends decided to have a word with Roel's parents and give Roel a chance to be part of the team.

The coach met Roel's parents and Roel's wheelchair was re-fitted. He was asked to practise. Roel practised very hard. Soon, he was able to become a part of Tanmay's team for all their friendly matches.

Roel was ecstatic! He could not thank Tanmay enough for helping his dreams come true.

Think and Say

Your friend who cannot run very fast wants to play carrom and you want to play hide and seek. What would you do?

Remember

- Make friendship with a specially-abled child.
- Everyone is good at something. Praise them for it.
- Look for good qualities in people and respect them for those.
- Everyone is equal. Treat everyone with respect.

Figure out

Tick (✓) the correct answers.

1. How did Roel spend his free time?
   a. He watched Tanmay and his friends play. ☐
   b. He sat sulking in his room. ☐
2. Roel was ecstatic when he could play basketball as part of the team because
   a. he could now beat Tanmay at basketball. ☐
   b. he had never thought that he could play basketball as he used a wheelchair. ☐
3. Roel was allowed to play basketball because
   a. he practised and trained hard. ☐
   b. the coach took pity on him. ☐
4. Roel was in a wheelchair. Was it right to let Roel play in the team?
   a. It did not matter that Roel was in a wheelchair because he played basketball well. ☐
   b. Roel was a liability to the team. He should have not been made part of the team. ☐
5. Who supported Roel to make his dream come true?
   a. Tanmay, his friends, the coach and Roel's parents supported him. ☐
   b. The school principal and other staff supported him. ☐

B. Answer these questions orally.

1. What did Roel dream of doing?
2. How did Tanmay know that Roel was skilled enough to play friendly matches?
3. Do you think Tanmay was right to support Roel? Give reasons for your answers.

Relate

Draw a  for the best answer.

1. Sam has only one hand. He goes to school in your bus and has difficulty in boarding the bus. What would you do?
   a. I would board the bus and start talking to my friends.
   b. I would help Sam board the bus.
2. Your friends are making fun of your classmate Manisha's old and faded uniform. What would you do?
   a. I would join the fun.
   b. I would stand up for Manisha and stop others from making fun of her.
3. Alok stutters when he speaks. The teacher asks him to read aloud in class so that he gains some confidence. What would you do?
   a. I would snigger and make rude remarks.
   b. I would be silent and listen to him. Later on, I would appreciate his effort.
4. During a practice session for your school play, you find that Vivek is standing in a corner, watching everyone else practise. You know that Vivek cannot hear properly and uses a hearing aid. Would you ask him to be a part of your play?
   a. Yes, I would. We would just need to practise a little harder to help Vivek.
   b. No, I would not. If Vivek can't hear properly, then our performance would suffer because of him.

Workout

Colour these pictures. Look at them carefully about the differences that you notice in them.

Happiness Box

1. **Being different is good. Make a booklet titled 'It's All Right to be Different'. The first four pages have been done for you. Copy these pages and add four more to the booklet.**

It's all right to have some teeth missing.

It's all right to be of a different colour.

It's all right to wear glasses.

It's all right to be adopted.

2. Look at the images given below. Are these images different? Tick (✓) the correct answer.

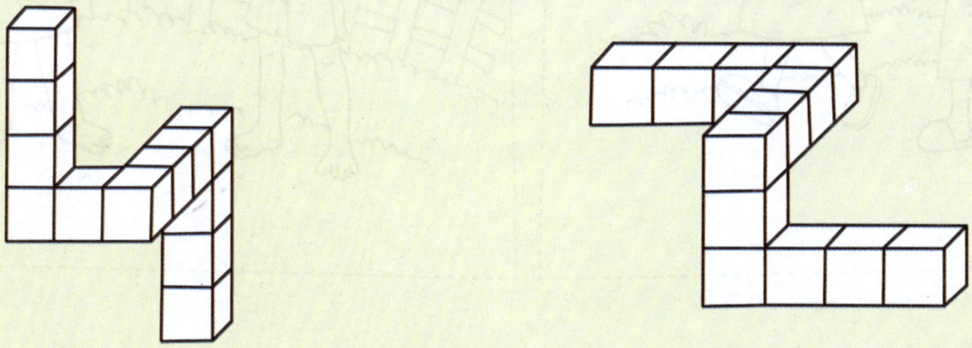

Yes ☐ No ☐

Teaching tips

- Talk about the ways in which people are treated with inequality. You may talk about issues such as social status, financial status and gender bias.
- Highlight instances where someone has established equality for themselves, or their people.
- Talk about Apartheid and the struggle to abolish it.
- Speak about various skills that each child in the class has.

2. Emperor Ping

Discuss

Look at the pictures. Talk about them in the class.

Read along

Once there was an Emperor who did not have an heir. When it was almost time for him to step down, he decided that he would choose the next emperor from his people. According to him, integrity was the most important virtue. Therefore, he wanted the next emperor to have this quality.

The Emperor knew that choosing the next emperor from his vast empire would be very difficult. He kept thinking of how the right person could be selected. After a lot of thought, he made a plan. He called everyone who wanted to become an emperor and gave each of them a seed and a pot. Then he said, 'Two months from now, the person who grows the best flower will become the Emperor!'

Among the people who received the seed and the pot, there was a young man called Ping. Ping was very good at gardening and was happy that the Emperor had set such an easy task. He took care of the seed and watered it every day. He gave it special care and attention. He even mixed in the best fertilizers possible. But to his dismay, nothing grew from the seed, let alone a flower.

Soon, the two-month period was over and it was time to meet the Emperor. Ping carried his empty pot with him and stood in the queue of people who had come to show the flowers to the Emperor. When he saw the beautiful flowers that people were carrying with them, he felt really disheartened.

The Emperor looked at each flower. He did not say a word as he passed the beautiful flowers. When he came upon Ping's empty pot, he looked up at Ping and smiled. He said, 'You will be the next Emperor, young man'. Saying this, the Emperor led Ping to the stage.

Think and Say

You are working on a project that you need to submit tomorrow. Just a little bit of work is left on the project. Your friend calls to chat with you. What would you do?

Confused, everybody looked at the Emperor for an explanation. The Emperor said, 'Honesty is important. Not only in words do we need to be honest, but our actions should show honesty too. The seeds that I had given everybody were boiled seeds. They were not meant to grow. But, these flowers in your pots prove that all of you have been dishonest.'

The people gaped at the Emperor in shock. The Emperor then continued, 'This young man here is the only person who has integrity and is honest. He did not replace the seed that I had given him. Therefore, he is the only one who deserves to be the Emperor'. Saying this, the Emperor crowned Ping the next ruler.

Emperor Ping, with his integrity and honesty, ruled the kingdom successfully for a long time.

Remember

- Integrity is a very important quality to have.
- Always be truthful.
- Although being honest requires a lot of courage, do not shy away from it.
- Have integrity not just in your words but in your actions too.

Figure out

Tick (✓) the correct answers.

1. Ping took special care of the seed,

   a. but no flower grew in his pot. ☐

   b. and as a result, a beautiful flowering plant grew from the seed. ☐

2. The fact that so many pots had flowers in them showed that
   a. Ping did not know how to grow plants.
   b. the others had all replaced the seeds, when they would not grow.
3. The Emperor created this test to see
   a. who had the integrity to keep the original seed.
   b. who was smart enough to plant a new seed.
4. The Emperor knew everybody was dishonest because
   a. they had flowers growing in their pots.
   b. they were smiling.
5. The Emperor chose Ping as the next emperor because
   a. Ping proved that he was a man of integrity.
   b. Ping had grown the most beautiful flower.

B. Answer these questions orally.

1. Why do you think Ping did not replace the seed given to him by the Emperor?
2. Was the task set by the Emperor a true test of integrity?
3. What do you think would have happened had Ping also replaced the seed like all the others?

Relate

Draw a ☺ for the best answer.

1. Your teacher has asked you to work on a project on your own. What would you do?
   a. I would take the help of my parents or older brother or sister to work on the project.
   b. I would work on the project the best way I could, on my own, and submit it.

2. Your parents have told you that you can play games on the computer for an hour. However, they are too busy to check on you. What would you do?
   a. I would shut the computer down after an hour. ◯
   b. I would continue playing as there is no one to check on me. ◯
3. You want to go for a movie with your friends. You know that your parents are not very comfortable about allowing you to go with friends for a movie. What would you do?
   a. I would tell them that I am going out for lunch and go watch movie with my friends. ◯
   b. I would try to convince them to allow me to go for the movie. ◯

Workout

Read some good qualities and tick the ones you think you possess. Be honest and leave out the qualities you think you don't possess. Don't worry, you can always work on those.

Bold – I do not shy away from challenges.

Content – I am happy with what I have.

Diligent – I work hard to complete the task I take up.

Empathetic – I feel other people's joys and sorrows.

Forgiving – I forgive people.

Giving – I share and give happily.

Humble – I don't show off my achievements.

Joyful – I enjoy the simple joys of life.

Kindhearted – I care for the needs of others.

Loyal – I am there for my family and friends in their good and bad times.

Neighbourly – I respect my neighbours.

Patient – I am patient with others.

Responsible – I do things to the best of my ability.

Self-controlled – I practise self-control in my words and actions.

Thankful – I am thankful for all I have.

Unwavering – When I set my mind to do something, I do it.

Happiness Box

1. **Count Your Cookies**

   Take a jar. Make seven cardboard cookies. Over the course of one week, put one cookie in the jar for one good deed done each day. If you do something wrong, take one cookie out. If you didn't do any good or bad deeds on a day, neither put in nor take out any cookies.

   At the end of the week, count and see how many cookies you have earned. Aim for all seven!

2. **Using the letters in the three words given below and make as many words as you can.**

   Integrity Honesty Truth

Teaching tips

- Emphasize on honesty in actions.
- Talk about integrity and how important it is in all walks of life.
- Have a discussion on being honest to oneself.

3. The Community Effort

Discuss

Look at the pictures. Talk about them in the class.

Read along

The global goal, Sustainable Cities and Communities, aims to makes cities and communities safe, clean and sustainable. Waste management is an important aspect of this goal, which can only be achieved when everyone from the community participates in cleaning initiatives. Let us see how Ashima and Ashish started a campaign to clean their park and make it safe too.

Ashima and Ashish were playing in the park, when they saw an old man trip over something and fall. They ran to help the old man. When they had made sure that he was not hurt, they went to see what he had tripped over. They saw a pile of wrappers, ice cream sticks, dry leaves, dead flowers and a deflated ball.

'Look here, Ashima. This is the pile of waste on which the old man tripped', said Ashish.

'Yes, this is so sad. People eat ice cream and throw the wrappers and sticks around. All this piles up and can hurt people', said Ashima, shaking her head.

'Hmm... I have an idea Ashima! Let's clean the park and educate people about the bad effects of littering'. said Ashish excitedly.

'But, how can we do this?' asked Ashima.

'Every day, before we start playing, we will go around in groups and clean sections of the park. After that, for fifteen minutes, we

will talk to people. We will ask everyone to respect the park and keep it clean', said Ashish.

'We can also make posters and put them up in the park so that people remember', said Ashima.

'Now, you are thinking!' said Ashish. Together they ran back to the group with which they were playing.

They told other children in their group about cleaning the park. All the children agreed. The next day, Ashish and Ashima reached a little early. They were carrying chart papers, colours, rulers, scissors and old magazines. All the children got together and made posters. The next day, they divided themselves in to groups and first cleaned the park. As it was quite dirty, it took all their allotted time. The third day, again the children went around cleaning the park and stuck posters all around the park.

By now, all the other people in the park had become quite curious. They wanted to know what these children were trying to do. On the fourth day, after cleaning the park, the children went to different groups of people and talked to them about caring for the park.

Everybody was so impressed by the efforts of the children that they readily offered help. In fact, people joined hands with the children to clean the park and educate others.

Think and Say

You see a small child trampling the flowers while playing in the park. What would you do?

In just a few days, people understood the importance of keeping the park clean and respecting its beauty. In fact, the children played happily now as their toys didn't get dirty. Old people walked more freely as they were no longer scared of tripping over piles of rubbish. It was the cleanest park you had ever seen because the people using it kept it so.

Remember

- Be a responsible member of your community.
- Keep your surroundings neat and clean.
- If you see someone damaging public property, talk to them and explain why it is wrong.
- Respect nature and take care of it.

Figure out

A. Tick (✓) the correct answers.

1. Ashima and Ashish ran to help the old man because
   a. they were responsible children. ☐
   b. they knew the old man. ☐
2. The fact that so many pots had flowers in them showed that
   a. people made the park dirty. ☐
   b. the old man tripped and fell. ☐
3. Ashima knew that it was important to remind people to clean the park. For this, she suggested that
   a. a meeting should be held every day. ☐
   b. campaign posters for cleaning the park should be made. ☐
4. The other people helped because
   a. they were inspired by the children. ☐
   b. they had nothing else to do. ☐

5. The children took it upon themselves to
   a. clean the park and educate others to do the same.
   b. jump around in the park.

B. Answer these questions orally.

1. How did the children take care of the park?
2. Why did it take the children the entire allotted time to clean the park on the first day?
3. How did the other people in the park react to the children's efforts?

Relate

Draw a ☺ for the best answer.

1. Your society is running a 'No Plastic Bags' drive. You see the shopkeeper in your colony giving out plastic bags secretly. What would you do?
   a. I would inform my parents or the welfare association of my society.
   b. I would ignore the shopkeeper and go to the park to play.
2. You see an old couple eating peanuts while walking and throwing the shells on the road. What would you do?
   a. I would greet them and go on my way.
   b. I would request them not to throw the shells on the road.
3. There is a 'Do not pluck flowers' sign in the park. You see a young child plucking flowers from there. What would you do?
   a. I would scold the child.
   b. I would politely ask the child not to pluck flowers.

Workout

A group of children at the zoo are teasing animals. Write what you would say to them.

....

....

....

....

....

....

Happiness Box

1. Follow the instructions to make origami tulips. Decorate your room with a bunch of these.

You need

- Origami paper of various colours
- Coloured ice cream sticks

Steps

1. 

Keep the paper's coloured side up. Fold it in half and then fold it again in half. Crease well and open.

2. 

Turn the paper's white side up. Fold diagonally in both the directions. Crease well and open.

3. 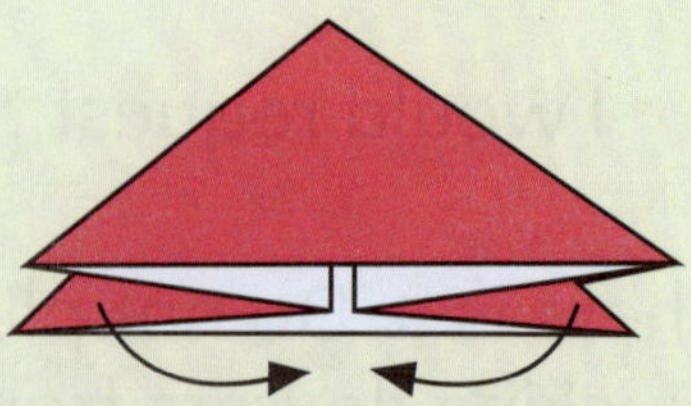

Hold the centre points of both the sides of the paper and bring inwards towards the centre of the bottom line. Flatten it.

4.

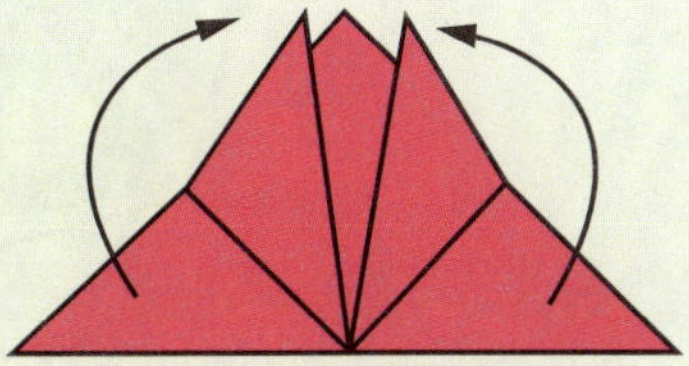

Fold the bottom corners of the front flap to touch the top. Turn and repeat for the back flap.

5.

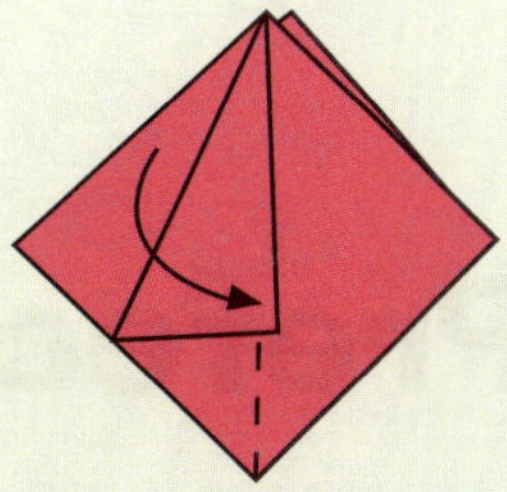

Just like you turn the pages of a book, fold the front flap to the right. Turn and repeat for the back flap.

6.

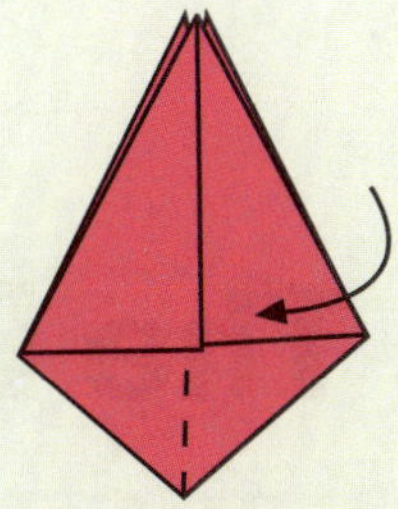

Insert the right flap in the left flap as far as it goes. Turn and repeat.

7.

Flatten the flower. Inflate it by blowing air into the hole at its base.

8.

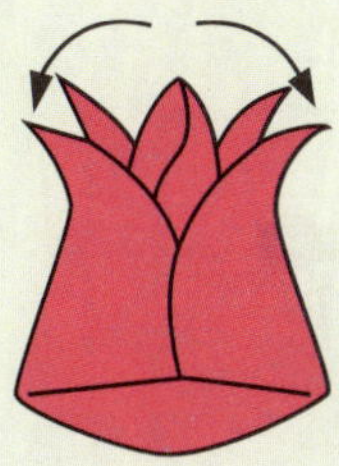

Open each petal out carefully as shown.

Repeat steps to make more such tulips. Bunch them together.

9.

Insert a coloured ice cream stick in the hole.

2. Read about the Chipko Movement. You can search the Internet for it. Write how people saved their trees and communities during this movement.

3. Hold a class debate on the following topic:

A Green World Is a Clean World

Teaching tips

- Talk to the students about the importance of nature in our daily lives.
- Tell students how all of us are responsible for the national property.
- Ensure that students understand the value of civic property.
- Tell the class how different life would be without civic property.

4. The Best Prefect

Discuss

Look at the pictures. Talk about them in the class.

Read along

Aahana and Ayesha were the best of friends. They loved each other and stood by each other during good and bad times.

When they reached the fifth grade, Aahana was made the Junior School Prefect. Ayesha was very proud of Aahana. She knew that her friend was the best prefect in the school.

It so happened that over the weekend, Ayesha forgot to cut her nails. But she was not that bothered as it was Aahana who checked the students' nails before the assembly. Being her best friend, Ayesha was sure that Aahana would let her go.

At the assembly, when it was time to get their nails checked, Ayesha confidently showed her hands to Aahana. Aahana, seeing her friend's long nails, said, 'Ayesha, your nails are quite long. I am afraid you will have to take a round of the playground'.

Think and Say

Your friend has fallen down and scraped her knee and you are heading for your debate competition. What would you do?

Ayesha was shocked to hear this. She felt really hurt. She left the line quietly and started running around the playground. She was really angry with Aahana. Aahana also felt bad that she had to do this to Ayesha.

When Ayesha reached home, her mother asked her how her day was. She started crying and said, 'Mother, today Aahana punished me. She made me a take a round of the playground because my nails were long. Can you believe it? I am her best friend. Why did she do this to me?'

Mother smiled and said, 'Ayesha, don't feel bad. Aahana was just doing her duty. When you are in a position of responsibility, you have to treat everyone equally, even if they are your friends. Aahana was being fair. Instead of crying over it, you should support her.'

The next day at school, Ayesha went to Aahana. 'Aahana, please forgive me. I thought you were being mean to me on purpose. But, Mother is right. You have to be fair. I am happy that you were able to see beyond our friendship and act responsibly. After all, you are the best prefect in school,' she said.

Aahana hugged Ayesha. 'I felt horrible about punishing you. Thank you for understanding, Ayesha'.

Remember

- Understand your responsibilities.
- Behave responsibly in class and at home.
- Do not damage any property that belongs to others.
- Take special care of the things that you have borrowed and return them in time.
- Take care of the library in your school and the books in it.

Rules and Laws

Personal Safety

A law is a rule or set of rules for good behaviour which is considered right and important by the majority of people. Rules are made for safety, health and efficiency. As children we think that rules are made only for us. However, rules are made for grown-ups too. When grown-ups break the law, they are handled by police and punished by the court. Sometimes, grown-ups are sent to jail for breaking a law. It is important to know that our parents, teachers or caregivers may punish us for breaking a rule, but no one should physically attack us. If anyone does so, they are violating a child's rights, which is punishable under law.

Figure out

A. Tick (✓) the correct answers.

1. Aahana was made the school prefect. How did Ayesha feel?
   a. Ayesha was proud of Aahana.
   b. Ayesha was jealous of Aahana.
2. Ayesha was sure that Aahana would not punish her for her long nails. Instead, Aahana punished her. Did Aahana do the right thing?
   a. Yes, as prefect, it was Aahana's responsibility to check Ayesha's nails.
   b. No, Aahana was taking undue advantage of her position.
3. Should those in positions of power help their friends when the friends break the rules?
   a. No, it is the responsibility of the person in power to treat everybody equally and fairly.
   b. Yes, after all, friends should always help each other out.
4. Had you been in Aahana's position, which of these would you have done?
   a. I would have helped Ayesha.
   b. I would have punished Ayesha, so she would understand where she had gone wrong.
5. Which of these qualities describe Aahana.
   a. Biased, dishonest, and undisciplined
   b. Fair, honest, and disciplined

B. Answer these questions orally.

1. How did Ayesha feel when Aahana punished her?
2. How did Aahana feel when she punished Ayesha?
3. After Mother explained Aahana's actions to Ayesha, did their friendship break?

Relate

Draw a 🙂 for the best answer.

1. You are the last one to leave the computer lab. What would you do?
   a. I would leave the computer switched on. ◯
   b. I would switch off the computer, the lights and the fans of the computer lab and then leave. ◯

2. You forget to get your paint box. The art teacher asks you to use the school paint box. When you search for it, you cannot find it in the cupboard. What would you do?
   a. I would search the entire cupboard and leave it disorganized. ◯
   b. I would be careful while searching through the cupboard and leave it organized. ◯

3. At the end of the sports period, you are very tired. However, you know that you need to put the basketball back in its proper place. What would you do?
   a. I would quietly leave the basketball on the floor. ◯
   b. I would make the effort to put the basketball back where it belongs. ◯

4. Five minutes of your lunch break are left. You know that if you start a game now, you will not be able to finish it. What would you do?
   a. I would not start a new game and start heading towards my classroom. ◯
   b. I would start a new game, finish it and go late for class. ◯

Workout

Find a newspaper report of any natural disaster that has occurred recently. Study the clipping carefully and answer the questions.

1. Where did you get the news of the disaster from?
2. Which disaster does the newspaper report talk about?

3. When did the disaster occur?
4. Where did the disaster occur?
5. Summarize the newspaper report in 200 words.
6. List three things that you would do if you found yourself in the middle of such a disaster.

Happiness Box

1. Let's Make a Six-Petal Duty Card

You need

- Coloured chart paper
- Bold markers
- Scissors
- Glue
- Your photograph

Steps

1. Make a six-petal flower using the cardboard or the coloured chart paper.
2. Cut it out.
3. In the centre, paste your photograph. On the petals, write any six responsibilities that you have taken up in and around your home.

2. Write two synonyms for the word responsibility. What does responsibility mean to you?

....

....

Teaching tips

- Talk to the students about the importance of being fair.
- Tell students that they should always be good people and help their friends become good people. That is why, while in a position of responsibility, punishing their friends if they are wrong is all right.
- Explain that those in positions of power have to act responsibly.

5. Happy Birthday, Grandmother

Discuss

Look at the pictures. Talk about them in the class.

Read along

'Hey Sheenu, I have an idea!' cried Shampa as she ran towards her sister.

Sheenu asked, 'What is it?'

Shampa put her arms around Sheenu and said, 'You know that Grandmother's 90th birthday is approaching. Let's plan a party for her. We'll discuss with Mother, Father and all our cousins. I am sure that they will help us.'

'That's great! Let us ask all our cousins to perform a dance routine for her. That will be really exciting!' said Shampa gleefully.

Sheenu and Shampa reached home and went straight to their mother. 'Mother, we want to plan a party for Grandmother's 90th birthday. We want to have all Grandmother's favourite things like chips, cutlets, *halwa*, *pav bhaji* and a huge cake', said Sheenu.

'And we want to call all Grandmother's friends too', added Shampa.

'That's a nice idea. We should start work on it immediately', Mother smiled and encouraged the sisters.

The sisters then talked to their father and their cousins. Everybody was happy to contribute in whatever way they could to make the party a huge success.

Soon, it was Grandmother's birthday. What a surprise she got when she saw all her friends in the house. People did not stop pouring in.

Her friends and all other family members came laden with gifts for her. She could not believe her eyes! Sheenu's and Shampa's cousins presented a dance routine for her. At the end, Grandmother also joined in. After that, she cut the cake to loud cheers from the family. She was so happy.

Think and Say

Your sister has been studying really hard for her examinations. You know that it is time for her evening snack, but she has not come to the table. What would you do?

When she asked who had planned the party, the cousins pushed Sheenu and Shampa to the front of the group. They smiled, put their arms around all their cousins and said, 'All of us planned your birthday together, Grandmother'.

Remember

- Take the initiative to learn something new every day.
- Be more forthcoming and help people.
- Taking initiative can sometimes be the reason why a project gets completed.

Figure out

A. Tick (✓) the correct answers.

1. Should Sheenu and Shampa have waited for someone else to plan Grandmother's birthday party?
   a. No, they could easily plan it themselves. ☐
   b. Yes, after all, it was not as if it was their birthday. ☐
2. What did Sheenu want to surprise her grandmother with?
   a. A birthday gift ☐
   b. A surprise birthday party attended by all her friends and family. ☐
3. Whom do Sheenu and Shampa ask to prepare a dance routine?
   a. Their cousins ☐
   b. Grandmother's friends ☐
4. Everybody contributed happily to Grandmother's party because
   a. they had no choice and had to contribute to the party. ☐
   b. they wanted the party to be a success. ☐
5. Who got the idea of celebrating Grandmother's birthday?
   a. Sheenu and Shampa ☐
   b. Everyone in the family ☐

B. Answer these questions orally.

1. Why did Sheenu and Shampa plan a party for Grandmother's birthday?
2. What did Sheenu and Shampa tell Mother they wanted for Grandmother's birthday party?
3. Why was Grandmother surprised on her birthday?

Relate

Draw a 🙂 for the best answer.

1. You come across a wonderful idea to have a small library in your class. What would you do?
   a. I would not tell my teacher or classmates about my idea because there is already a library in the school. ◯
   b. I would talk to my teacher about it and collect old books from my classmates. This way, everyone in the class could exchange books and read them. ◯
2. You see that your little sister has slept without keeping her toys back in the cupboard. What would you do?
   a. I would put her toys back in the cupboard and tidy up her play area. ◯
   b. I would ignore the strewn toys and go to sleep too. ◯
3. Your sister has wanted to watch a particular movie for a long time. As you are scrolling through the TV schedule, you notice that it is finally being aired the next day. What would you do?
   a. I would quickly go and tell my sister about it. She would be really excited. ◯
   b. I would tell her when I see her. After all, it is not being aired till tomorrow. ◯

Workout

Learn how to breathe properly. Practise this exercise for five minutes daily.

- The first step would be to breathe through the nose.

- Sit up straight and exhale completely.
- Inhale while relaxing the stomach muscles. Feel your body responding.
- Inhale as deeply as you can. You will feel your chest and rib cage expand.
- Hold your breath for a few seconds.
- Start exhaling as slowly as possible.
- While exhaling, relax your chest and rib cage. At the same time, pull your stomach in.
- Close your eyes and feel yourself breathing.

Happiness Box

1. Make a diet chart for yourself. Keep in mind the right foods that you should eat to grow. From the box below, pick up the right food for the right meal to fill the chart.

	Brilliant Breakfast	Lovely Lunch	Super Snacks	Dynamite Dinner
Sunday				
Monday				
Tuesday				
Wednesday				
Thursday				
Friday				
Saturday				

chicken curry | *pav bhaji* | sambar | roti | mixed dal

kachumber salad | parantha | pasta | *raita* | rajma rice

vegetable fried rice | kadhi rice | pulao | idli | fish curry

moong sprouts | fruit | daliya | custard | vegetable chowmein

kala chana masala | *karela aalu* | sandwich | laddoo | *khichdi*

coconut *burfi* | *shahi paneer* | lemonade | ice cream | doughnut

2. Communication is not limited to speaking. Hand signs can also be a way to communicate. Decode the secret message sent using the sign chart given below.

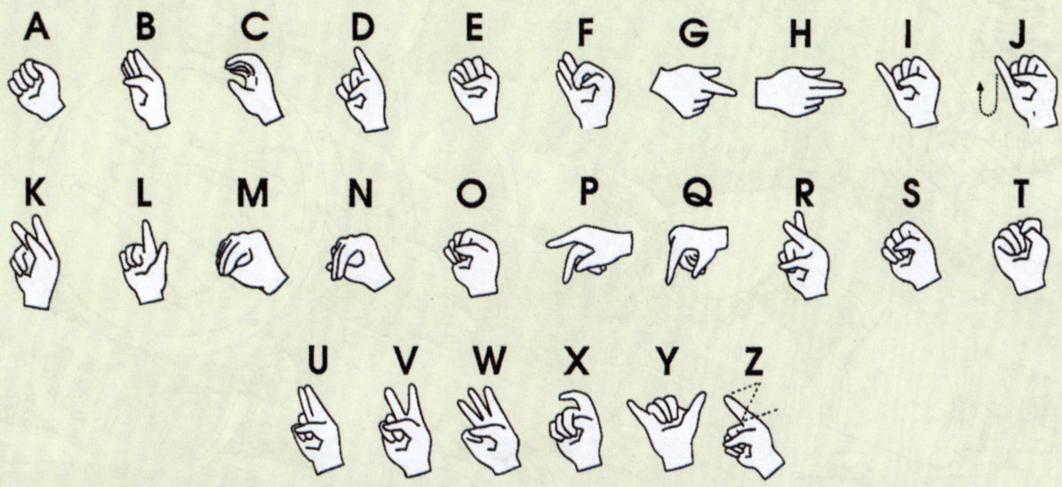

Secret Message

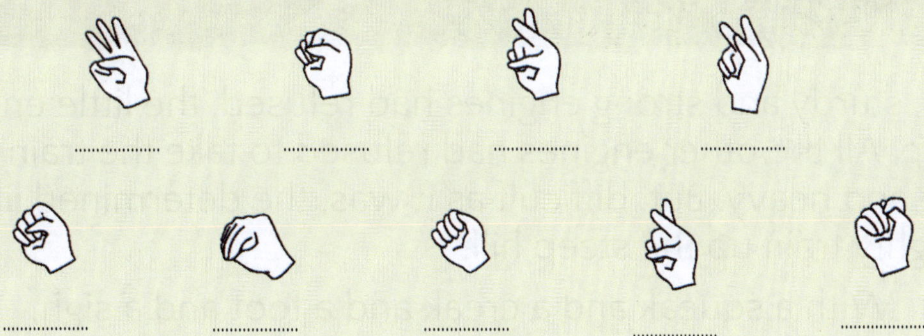

Teaching tips

- Talk to the students about the importance of having ideas and implementing them.
- Give students multiple situations like grandparents' 50th wedding anniversary, Yoga Day, pet's birthday, World Earth Day and other similar situations and ask them what they would do in each. This would enable cross-disciplinary thinking and would also encourage them to think and take the initiative.

6. Dr Glen Cunningham

Discuss

This picture is of the little engine that could. Talk about it in class.

While the big, sturdy and strong engines had refused, the little engine had offered to help. All the other engines had refused to take the train up because it was so long and heavy. But, difficult as it was, the determined little engine pulled the mighty train up the steep hill.

With a squeak and a creak and a toot and a sigh,
With an extra hope and an extra try,
He would not stop—now he neared the top—
And strong and proud he cried out loud,
"I think I can, I think I can, I think I can!"

Do you think the little engine could do this because it used the strength of its mind?

Read along

An eight-year-old boy was responsible for coming to school early to warm the room before his teacher and classmates arrived. This, he did by starting the old-fashioned, pot-bellied coal stove every day.

One morning, when the teachers and the other students arrived, they found that the schoolhouse was on fire. They also saw the little boy lying unconscious in the flames. They dragged the boy out and took him to a nearby county hospital. He had major burns over the lower half of his body.

From his bed, the burned, semi-conscious boy faintly heard the doctor talking to his mother. The doctor was telling his mother that her son would not make it as the terrible fire had almost destroyed the lower half of his body.

But the brave boy didn't want to die. He made up his mind that he would live. Somehow, he did live. After some days, he heard the doctor and his mother speaking quietly, again. This time, the doctor told his mother that the little boy would not be able to use his legs at all and would be a cripple all his life.

Once again, the brave boy made up his mind. He would not be a cripple. He wanted to walk. He would walk. Unfortunately, he had no sensation or movement in his body, from waist down. His thin legs just dangled there, complete but lifeless.

Soon, he was released from the hospital. When he wasn't in bed, he was confined to a wheelchair. His mother massaged his thin legs every day hoping that someday, they would feel something. But, nothing happened.

One sunny day, his mother wheeled him out into the yard to get some fresh air. That day, instead of sitting there, the boy threw himself from the chair. He pulled himself across the grass, dragging his legs behind him.

He worked his way to the white picket fence bordering their garden. With great effort, he raised himself up on the fence. Then, he began dragging

Think and Say

You have failed at Math in both the term tests. Now, the third term tests are to begin. You don't want to study Math as you are sure you will fail again. What would you do?

himself along the fence, all the while, determined that he would walk. He started to do this every day. There was nothing he wanted more than to have life in those legs.

Ultimately, through his daily massages and his unwavering determination, he developed the ability to stand up. Slowly, he started walking haltingly, then walked by himself, and then, to run. It took him twenty-two months to achieve this.

He ran for the sheer joy of running and was one of the best athletes of the time. After passing high school, he attended the Kansas University, where he was a part of the track team.

He took part in the 1932 Olympics, where he ran the 1500 m race. He finished fourth which was more than anyone expected him to achieve. In 1936, he was voted the 'Most Popular Athlete' by his fellow athletes.

In 1938, in Madison Square Garden, this determined young man, who was not expected to live, ran the world's fastest mile!

In 1940, he retired from his running career and started teaching at the Cornell College in Iowa. He also ran the Youth Ranch for troubled children in Kansas, USA. This man, who helped more than 9,000 children, was Dr Glen Cunningham.

Remember

- Determination and success go hand in hand.
- Determination is an important factor in reaching your goals.
- Determination means doing something with a strong desire.
- If you are determined to achieve something, you will be able to do.

Figure out

A. Tick (✓) the correct answers.

1. The doctors said that the little boy would die but he lived because
   a. he was not that burnt. ☐
   b. he had made up his mind to do so. ☐

2. The little boy could not walk because
   a. he did not try hard.
   b. the fire had destroyed the lower part of his body.
3. The little boy dragged himself along the fence because
   a. he was determined to walk.
   b. he had no other way to pass his time.
4. The little boy started running
   a. for the sheer joy of running.
   b. so that he could run away from his home.

B. Answer these questions orally.

1. How did the little boy get burned?
2. How did the little boy force himself to walk?
3. Do you think that you can do anything if you set your mind to it?

Relate

Draw a 🙂 for the best answer.

1. You are a good swimmer and you have been winning competitions at school. A new boy who is also a good swimmer, joins your school. There is a swimming meet next month. What would you do?
   a. I would not take part in the swimming meet.
   b. I would take part in the swimming meet and train really hard for it.
2. You have been saving up for a some books that you what to buy. Suddenly, the price of the books increases. What would you do?
   a. I would save some more money so that I buy them.
   b. I would spend the money on chocolates.
3. Your friend has been preparing for the upcoming sports day for over four months. However, you notice that he has stopped going for his training.

He says that he does not feel like training any more. What would you do?

a. I would tell him that it is all right to quit. He can do what he wants. ◯

b. I would encourage him and ask him to continue training so that he can perform well on the sports day. ◯

Workout

Write a brief biographical sketch of Dr Glen Cunningham. Include all the major events of his life.

Happiness Box

1. Make a graphic organizer. In each circle, write what determination means to you. Three have been done for you.

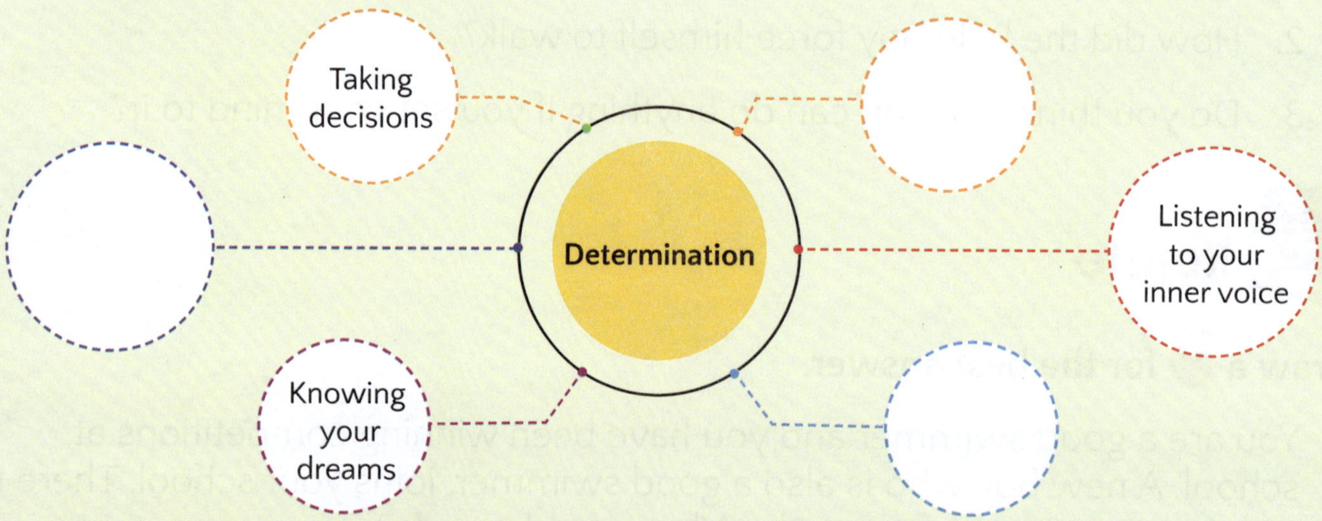

2. Write an advertisement for a teammate to work on a class project.

Your advertisement should list the qualities you want to have in your teammate. Share advertisement in class. Once you find a teammate, work with him or her for a month.

Teaching tips

- Highlight the importance of being focused in achieving any goal.
- Stress on how important it is to practise.
- Bring out the point that natural talent can go waste if not honed by hard work and determination.

Happiness Activity

We use electronic devices such as laptops, mobile phones and tablets.

Tick the things that you should do while using mobile phones.

We should keep our phones on silent mode when we meet someone. ☐

We should first ask the person we call if it is a good time to talk to them. ☐

We should play on our mobile phones while in restaurants or in family functions. ☐

We should talk softly on the phone when in a public place or while using public transport. ☐

We should peep into other people's phone screens. ☐

We should eat while using our phones. ☐

Colour the poster. Circle the pictures that show the incorrect way of using electronic devices.

Samar loves playing games on the mobile. Help him reach the games folder through the icon maze on his phone screen.

Project I : The Giving Cycle

During our lifetime, we give something and receive something. This is a two-way cycle. Therefore, while it is important to be thankful for what we receive, it is also important not to boast of any help that we give others. Here are some tables for you to fill up. Write names of two people in each.

People I am Thankful To

Name		Reason to be Thankful
1.		
2.		
3.		

People and Actions I should not Boast About

Name		My Act of Kindness
1.		
2.		

People who Need More of my Support

Name		Reason They Need My Support
1.		
2.		

7. Sibling Love

Discuss

Tina and Amol's favourite time together is when they talk while swinging. Discuss all the things you think they might talk about.

You were an only child or
maybe you weren't,
Maybe you were playing with
your teddy bear named Bert.
When your father took you to
that hospital wing,
To see your mother, and you
found your younger sibling.
Maybe you wondered why
your sibling was so small,
But it didn't matter, it was your
sibling all in all.
And as you grew together, you
would laugh, play and sing,
Together, you would do
anything.

Read along

Shraman and his younger sister, Namita reached home from school. When Shraman opened the door, he heard the phone ring. He ran to pick it up. It was his mother. 'Shraman, I am stuck at the office. It will take me almost two hours to reach home. Could you please be good and take care of your little sister?' she asked.

'Sure Mother. Don't worry. I will take care of Namita. Bye!' promised Shraman and disconnected the call.

He turned to look for Namita, but she was nowhere to be seen. Shraman then remembered that he had run inside to attend the phone without seeing whether Namita had entered the house or not. He went to look for her and there she was, sitting among the plants, talking to them and watering them from her water bottle.

'Namita, come inside,' said Shraman, gently leading her inside the house. Once she was inside the house, Shraman locked the door. He then made her wash her face and hands and change her clothes. He then washed his own hands and face and changed his clothes. After that, he laid out lunch for both of them. Namita was a fussy eater. Still, Shraman lovingly made sure she finished her meal. Once they had eaten their lunch, he put the dirty utensils in the sink.

‘What would you like to do now, Namita?’ asked Shraman.

‘I want to go outside and play,’ said Namita.

It was quite hot outside. Shraman said, ‘You can play, but you will have to play inside. It is too hot outside. I will play with you. What do you want to play?’

Namita thought for a while and said that she would like to play carrom. So, Shraman got the carrom board and set it up. They played carrom for almost an hour.

‘Shraman *bhaiya*, I am tired. I want to sleep’, said Namita.

‘Sure Namita. Just a minute. Let me put this carrom board away and then we can sleep’, said Shraman. By the time he came back, Namita was lying on the sofa, fast asleep. Shraman smiled, got her favourite quilt and covered her with it.

Think and Say

Your mother is out for some work and your elder brother is studying. You want a snack from the kitchen. Would you disturb your brother for it?

Just then, Mother arrived. When she saw that the house was in perfect order, Namita was sleeping peacefully and both of them had had lunch, she was really impressed. She hugged Shraman and said, ‘I am really proud of you, Shraman. It seems that you have taken wonderful care of your sister and the house. This shows your love for your sister. You are a good elder brother. Thank you and I love you’.

Shraman was also happy that he had been able to take care of Namita.

Remember

- Help your siblings whenever you can.
- Take care of them whether they are older or younger than you.
- Make sure you spend some time with them every day.
- Keep the promises that you make to them.

Figure out

A. Tick (✓) the correct answers.

1. What did Shraman understand after talking to his Mother on the phone?
   a. Shraman understood that he had to take care of his sister. ☐
   b. Shraman understood that he had to open the door for Mother. ☐
2. In his hurry to pick up the phone, what did Shraman forget to do?
   a. Shraman forgot to change his clothes. ☐
   b. Shraman forgot to see if Namita had entered the house. ☐
3. Namita was a fussy eater. What did Shraman do?
   a. Shraman scolded her to make her finish her lunch. ☐
   b. Shraman lovingly made her finish her lunch. ☐
4. Was Shraman right in asking Namita to play inside?
   a. Yes, it was very hot outside. ☐
   b. No, she was a child, she could play in the heat if she wanted to. ☐
5. Mother was happy with Shraman because
   a. Shraman had taken care of Namita with love. ☐
   b. Shraman had picked up her phone. ☐
6. What did Mother see when she came home?
   a. That the house was in a mess ☐
   b. That the house was in perfect order ☐

B. Answer these questions orally.

1. Was Shraman a responsible brother?
2. Was Namita old enough to take care of herself?
3. Why was Shraman's mother late?

Relate

Draw a 🙂 for the best answer.

1. Your cousin has come over to stay with you. He wants to play outside and you want to play video games. What would you do?
   a. I would ignore him and play video games.
   b. I would go out and play with him for some time.
2. Your elder sister is studying hard for her examinations. She wants you to do some of her household chores. What would you do?
   a. I would tell her that I am too little to do any household chores.
   b. I would help her happily so that she gets more time to study.
3. You are getting late to go for a party. However, your mother isn't back from office as yet. Your younger sister will be left alone in the house if you leave. What would you do?
   a. I would go to the party only after my mom is back.
   b. I would leave for the party hoping that my mother came back soon.
4. Your younger brother wants to ride your cycle. Will you let him ride it?
   a. Yes, but I would make sure that he doesn't fall or hurt himself.
   b. No, the cycle is mine. I would not allow him to ride it.

Happiness Box

1. Paste photographs of any four of your siblings or cousins here.

Paste here	Paste here	Paste here	Paste here

Now, play this fun game with them the next time you are together.

Try to say this tongue twister together. Start out slow, and then fast. See how fast you can go without stopping.

I feel I feel a funny feel, a funny feel I feel. If you feel the feel I feel, you feel a funny feel.

2. Find out how well you know your sibling. Try naming the following without asking them.

Your sibling's favourite:

Colour Food TV Show Sport Hobby

2. Try this brainteaser with your family.

1. Ask them to think of a number.
2. Subtarct 2 from that number and multiply the answer by 3.
3. Add 12 to the answer they got and further divide it by 3.
4. Add 5 to the number.
5. Subtract the original number from the answer.
6. Close your eyes and pretend to concentrate hard. Then, slowly 'guess' the number.
7. Tell them that the number they are left with is 7. Amazing, isn't it?

Teaching tips

- Tell students that there are many ways in which they can show love for their brothers and sisters.
- Small things like giving your sibling a glass of water when they are thirsty shows that you care for them.
- Tell them that it is important that they encourage their brothers and sisters when they are right and tell them when they are wrong.
- Talk to them about the love and responsibility that they must have for their brothers and sisters.

8. Rani's Gift

Discuss

Look at the pictures. Discuss them in class.

Read along

In a faraway town, lived two friends Rani and Geeta. Rani was a wealthy merchant's only daughter. Geeta was the daughter of their gardener. The girls loved each other dearly.

Every day, Geeta would come to call Rani to play. She would say, 'Let us go near the pond today, Rani. We can play on its banks'.

Often, Rani would say, 'Geeta let us play on the swings today'. The two girls would then laugh, giggle and play on the swings in Rani's garden.

It was Rani's birthday. She was really excited. She ran to her friend Geeta to invite her, 'Tomorrow is my birthday, Geeta, I will have a big party and you have to come'.

'Of course, I will come, dear friend', replied Geeta, happily.

Back home, Geeta started wondering what gift would make Rani the happiest. She asked her father, 'Father what should I give Rani as a gift? I want to give her the best present ever.'

At this, her father smiled, 'I have a lot of flowering plants. Choose the best-looking one and gift it to her'.

The next evening, Geeta arrived at Rani's house dressed in her best clothes. She saw that the house was decorated with lights, flower garlands and balloons. Some of their friends had already arrived.

'Happy birthday, Rani!' said Geeta, giving her a pot of beautiful white daisies. 'This is your birthday present, my friend'.

Think and Say

You notice that your elder sister talks quite rudely to your house help and other people who work for you. Even if they talk politely, she scolds them. What would you do?

'Is this for me? It is beautiful, Geeta! I love it', said Rani, taking the pot from Geeta.

'Mother, Father, Tina, Aditya, Sonam, everyone, come here!' Rani called loudly to all her friends. 'Look what Geeta has brought for me', said Rani. She showed everybody the potted plant happily.

'This is lovely, Geeta', said Aditya, admiring the flowers.

'A beautiful present indeed, Geeta. Was this your father's idea?' asked Rani's father.

'Yes, Uncle. But, I had also taken care of this plant along with my father. I'm glad that Rani likes it so much', said Geeta politely.

'In fact, amongst all the presents Rani has received, this is the prettiest,' said Sonam.

That night, Geeta was very happy. Geeta's father was happy too. He said to Geeta's mother, 'Rani's family has always treated us and our work respectfully. It's nice to see that their daughter also respects us'.

Empathy

Relationships

Empathy is the ability to share another person's feelings and emotions as if they were your own. To have a successful relationship with our loved ones, we need to understand and care about other peoples' needs and feelings. Empathy is the ability to imagine what life is like for another person. Without empathy we would act and behave according to our self-interest. We grow up in relationships with many people : parents, brothers and sisters, cousins, uncles and aunts, classmates, friends and neighbours. Empathy can help us to accept others, who may be very different from us. This can improve how we behave in situations of ethnic or cultural diversity.

Remember

- No work is small or big.
- Every kind of work has a special place.
- Help your parents with the household work.

Figure out

A. Tick (✓) the correct answers.

1. Geeta was the daughter of Rani's father's
   a. gardener.
   b. driver.
2. Geeta's father suggested
   a. an expensive gift for Rani.
   b. a flowering pot as a gift for Rani.
3. Geeta picked out the white daisies as a gift for Rani as
   a. she had herself taken care of the daisies.
   b. her father had told her to gift them to Rani.
4. Geeta's gift was special to Rani because
   a. Geeta had herself worked on it.
   b. Geeta was running short of flowers at her party.
5. Geeta's father was happy because
   a. he realized that Rani appreciated their hard work.
   b. he had one plant less to care for.

B. Answer these questions orally.

1. How did Geeta and Rani spend their time?
2. How was the house decorated?
3. Do you think that a pot of beautiful daisies make a nice gift?

Relate

Draw a ☺ for the best answer.

1. Your domestic help has not come. You see your mother doing the household work. What would you do?
   a. I would help my mother with the household work. ◯
   b. I would continue doing what I was doing. ◯
2. Your gardener asks you to help. What would you do?
   a. I would refuse to help him. ◯
   b. I would help him. ◯
3. You see that the fruit-seller who comes to your house has fallen down. What would you do?
   a. I would check if he was hurt. ◯
   b. I would ignore him and continue to do my own work. ◯

Workout

Unscramble the letters to find the names of certain professionals. Write a line explaining what each one of them does.

1. TSORNUATA ....
2. PNEACRTER ....
3. YSICIPHST ....
4. AMEFIRN ....

Happiness Box

1. Make a waste paper bin out of an old carton.

Materials needed

Old carton, coloured papers, glitter, stickers, sketch pens, glue

Steps

1. Cut the coloured paper to cover the carton.
2. Paste the coloured paper to cover all the sides of the carton.
3. Use glitter, stickers and colour pens to decorate the sides of the carton as you like.
4. Your waste paper bin is ready.

Use this bin for paper and dry waste only.

2. Write two synonyms for each these of words.

Wealthy Work Big Happy Different

Teaching tips

- Talk about how all work is important.
- Tell students how each person's work contributes to the community.
- Organize a community helpers meet where these helpers can come and talk to the students about their work.

9. The Statue of Wax

Discuss

Look at the pictures. Talk about them in class.

Read along

One day, Emperor Akbar called Birbal and said, 'Birbal, it is written in the books of Hinduism that when Lord Indra found his devoted elephant in pain, he himself rushed to help him. I can't understand the reason behind this. When Lord Indra had so many helpers, then why did he take the trouble to rush to his elephant, himself?'

Hearing this, Birbal was quiet for a moment. Then he said, '*Jahapanah*, I have understood your question, but I will answer it after a few days'.

A couple of days passed. Birbal planned something and spoke to one of his close friends, a royal helper. This helper was responsible for taking Akbar's grandson for a walk every day in the royal gardens. Sometimes, even Emperor Akbar joined them.

One day, after taking permission from the helper, Birbal took Akbar's grandson to a sculptor. Showing him to the sculptor, Birbal said, 'Make a wax statue which looks exactly like the child.'

Within a few hours the job was done to perfection. Birbal then dressed the statue in royal clothes and ornaments. Now, the statue looked just like Emperor Akbar's grandson.

Some days later, Birbal, having taken the royal helper into confidence, gave him Akbar's grandson's wax statue. 'Take this statue to the royal garden as usual. As Emperor Akbar approaches, you have to pretend to stumble on a rock beside the pond. Remember, you have to fall in such a way that you fall on the ground while the statue falls in the water. Do this while the Emperor is watching,' explained Birbal. Though puzzled, the helper did not question Birbal.

The helper did as he was told. Near the pond, he stumbled and fell, letting the statue slip into the water. He also ensured that when this happened, Akbar was watching.

Think and Say

A new girl has joined your class. You notice that a lot of people do not talk to her because of her oiled hair. What would you do?

The plan worked. On seeing his grandson fall into the water, Akbar panicked. Without giving any thought to who he was, he jumped into the pond to rescue his grandson. In the pond, he discovered the wax statue of his grandson. Angry, he looked at Birbal, who stood nearby, smiling. 'What kind of a joke is this Birbal? Why did you have to do such a thing?' thundered the Emperor.

Birbal said, '*Jahapanah*, you have so many helpers and attendants. Seeing your grandson in trouble, you did not call any of them and jumped into the pond yourself. Why did you do this?'

Emperor Akbar replied, 'I was so scared seeing my grandson in trouble that I could not think of anything else. I just jumped into the pond to help him'.

'You did exactly what Lord Indra had done, *Jahapanah*', said Birbal. 'God treats those loyal to him as his children. If they are in trouble, he helps them himself'.

Akbar understood and appreciated what Birbal meant and rewarded him.

Remember

- Never try to force your beliefs or customs on others.
- God is one. We just call him by different names.

Figure out

A. Tick (✓) the correct answers.

1. Emperor Akbar called Birbal and asked him
   a. why Lord Indra had taken the trouble to help his devoted elephant himself. ☐
   b. why Lord Indra prayed every day. ☐

2. Birbal said that he would explain everything to Akbar in a few days because
   a. he wanted to first plan out everything. ☐
   b. he did not have a ready answer. ☐

3. When Akbar saw his grandson fall in the pond,
   a. he jumped into the pond himself to help his grandson. ☐
   b. he ordered Birbal to jump in the pond to help his grandson. ☐

4. Akbar, the Emperor of the Mughal Empire, and Birbal, a member of his court, were
   a. friends who trusted each other. ☐
   b. two people who secretly disliked each other. ☐

5. Emperor Akbar understood that when you see your loved one in trouble,
   a. you run to help the person yourself. ☐
   b. you wait for somebody else to help the person. ☐

B. Answer these questions orally.

1. What question did Akbar ask Birbal?
2. Birbal took permission from the royal helper before taking Emperor Akbar's grandson with him. Do you think Birbal did the right thing?
3. Why did Akbar help his grandson himself?

Relate

Draw a 🙂 for the best answer.

1. When you are in trouble, what do you do?
   a. I would talk to different people and try to find a solution to my troubles. ◯
   b. I would feel sad and do nothing about it. ◯
2. You have a neighbour who belongs to another part of India. He has invited you to a celebration of one of his important festivals. What would you do?
   a. I would attend and enjoy the festival celebrations. ◯
   b. I would not go to the celebrations at all. ◯
3. You went to your friend's house where you were served a traditional dish. What would you do?
   a. I would taste it and then appreciate it. ◯
   b. I would appreciate the dish without tasting it. ◯
4. Your younger brother wants to ride your bicycle. Will you let him ride it?
   a. Yes, but I would make sure that he doesn't fall or hurt himself. ◯
   b. No, the cycle is mine. I would not allow him to ride it. ◯
5. You see that your mother has a lot of household work to do. What would you do?
   a. I would happily help her ◯
   b. I would ignore her ◯

Workout

Solve this crossword to find words from the story.

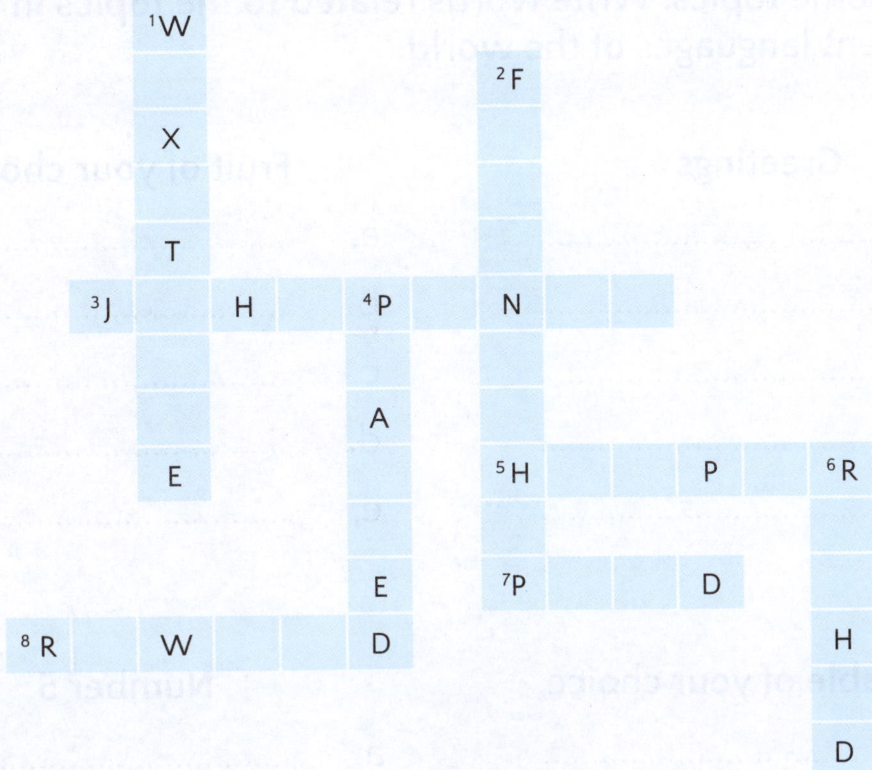

Clues

Across

3. The name, by which, Birbal addressed Emperor Akbar
5. People who are around the Emperor and do as he says
7. Where the wax statue fell
8. What Birbal got from Emperor Akbar for answering his query

Down

1. Birbal asked the sculptor to make this
2. The bond that Birbal had with the royal helper
4. Birbal .... a way to answer Emperor Akbar's question.
6. Lord Indra .... to help his devoted elephant.

Happiness Box

1. Make a collage of different dresses from all over India.
2. Here are some topics. Write words related to the topics in any five different languages of the world.

Greetings

a. ....

b. ....

c. ....

d. ....

e. ....

Fruit of your choice

a. ....

b. ....

c. ....

d. ....

e. ....

Vegetable of your choice

a. ....

b. ....

c. ....

d. ....

e. ....

Number 5

a. ....

b. ....

c. ....

d. ....

e. ....

Teaching tips

- Explain to the students that diversity is strength.
- Stress on how important it is to understand and respect different cultures.
- Show how all religions and cultures actually propound the same ideals and values.

10. Brave Akio

Discuss

Look at the pictures. Talk about them in class.

Read along

This story is from a beautiful village by the sea in Japan called Samrat.

In this village lived an old farmer called Akio. He lived all alone. His farmhouse was located high up on a plateau overlooking the village. Akio was a very kind, caring and thoughtful person. He was always concerned about his fellow villagers and their well-being.

One afternoon, Akio went near the seashore as he always did in the afternoons. The sky was overcast with clouds and the water was green. The sea was quite rough that day. Suddenly, to his horror, the tide changed its direction. Water started receding from the shore.

Akio at once understood what was happening. This was not new for him. He remembered how his village had once faced a similar situation. He also remembered how his grandfather's wit and courage had saved his family and many villagers. This had happened when he was a child.

'The sea will become a monster within a few minutes. I must warn the people who are on the shore to move away', thought Akio, alarmed.

Many villagers had come to the shore to see what was happening to the water. 'The water is going back! But why is this happening? Does anyone know?' asked a young girl. No one could answer her.

There were far too many people on the shore. It was impossible for Akio to warn everybody. Akio knew that there was hardly any time to tell the villagers what the sea was planning to do.

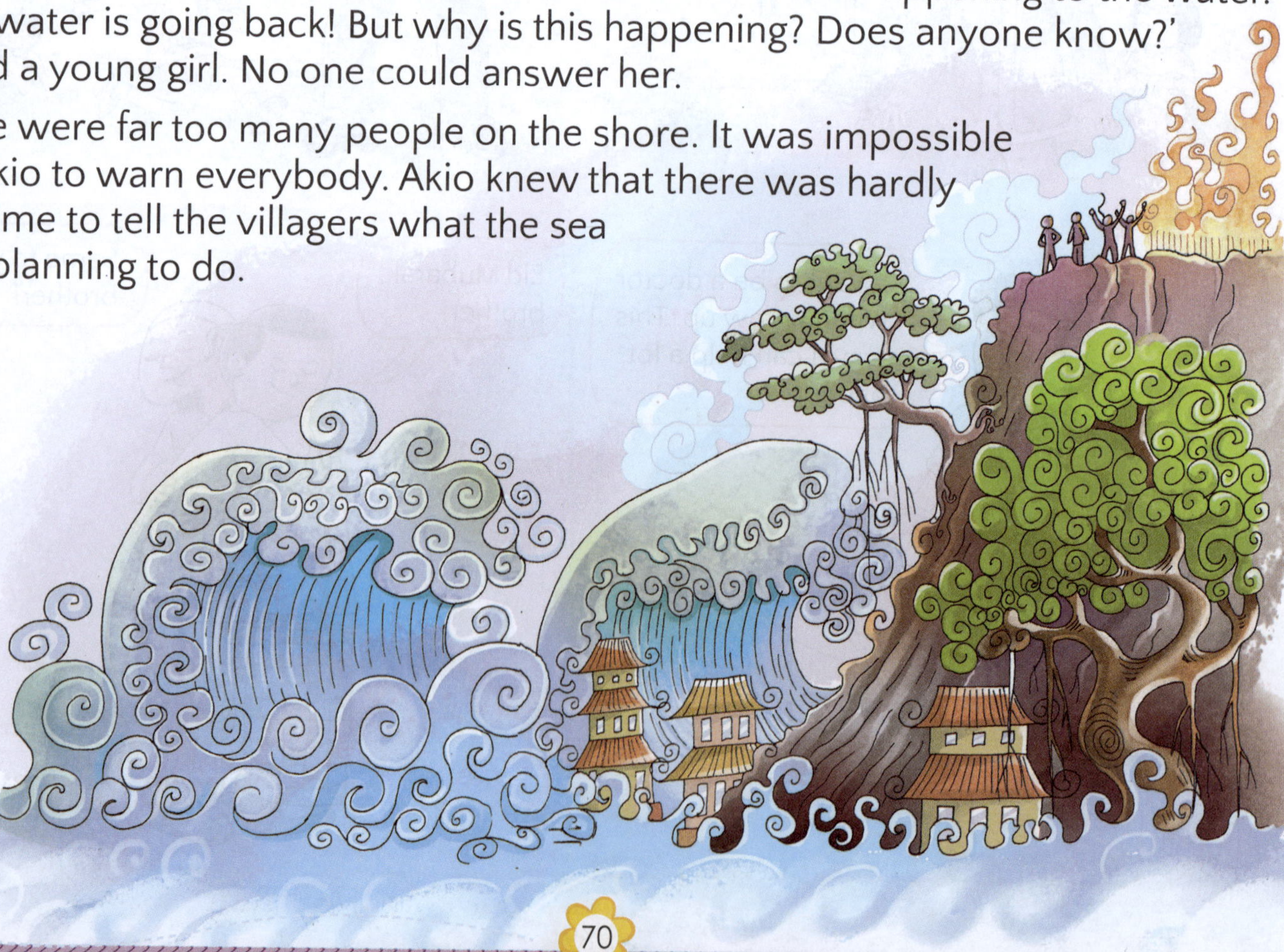

Thinking of a plan, Akio ran uphill to his farm as fast as his old, wobbly legs could carry him. The farm was the only thing Akio had. Without wasting time, Akio set fire to the rice growing on his field.

As soon as the fire started and smoke rose, all the villagers came running to help Akio. 'Run fast. Old Akio must be in trouble!' they cried. To their surprise, they saw Akio simply standing and watching his farm burn to ashes. 'Why! Akio is quite safe. Then, why is he watching his rice crop burn to ashes?' asked one man.

'Old Akio must have gone mad,' said another.

Just then, there was a loud noise. It was the sea. Tall waves of black water lashed the shore and their village was washed away in a second. The sea kept on roaring and the waves kept storming the shore for many hours. A tsunami had struck. Everything was finished . . . the crops, the huts and the cattle. But the people were alive because they were on the plateau with Akio.

It was then that they realized that Akio had saved their lives by burning his rice field. 'Akio is not mad. He has saved our lives!' gasped a woman.

'He knew that a tsunami was coming. He burnt his fields so that we would climb the plateau and move away from the shore', said a man.

Then all of them together raised Akio on their shoulders and shouted, 'Akio, you are a great man! Thank you for saving our lives'.

People remember Akio because of his sacrifice. Even today people tell tales of Akio's kindness and presence of mind to their children.

Remember

- We must be concerned for others around us.
- Sacrifice is also a form of love for others.
- If we give love, we receive love in return.
- Being concerned for others does not mean that we support their wrong actions.

Figure out

A. Tick (✓) the correct answers.

1. The old farmer Akio was known to be a
   a. kind, caring and a thoughtful person.
   b. rude and thoughtless person.
2. Akio's farm on the plateau high up helped Akio
   a. save his rice crop.
   b. save the life of the villagers.
3. When he looked at the sea, Akio was horrified as
   a. he knew what was about to happen.
   b. he could not understand why the sea was receding
4. Without wasting time,
   a. Akio had sacrificed the rice on his field.
   b. Akio filled water in his rice field.
5. The villagers realized that Akio
   a. was mad.
   b. was thoughtful and caring.

B. Answer these questions orally.

1. Why was the sea behaving strangely?
2. Why did Akio set fire to his only rice field?
3. Akio burnt his own rice crop to save the lives of the villagers. Do you think it was an act of love and concern for others?

Relate

Draw a 🙂 for the best answer.

1. You see that a hungry cat is mewling outside your house. What would you do?
   a. I would ask permission from Mother to give it some milk. ◯
   b. I would shoo it away. ◯

2. There is a fire in school. Everybody is moving out. Your differently-abled classmate is having difficulty in moving. What would you do?
   a. I would run out of the class thinking that the teachers would help him. ◯
   b. I would try to help my classmate. ◯

3. You are in a park. A stranger tries to steal your friend's toys. What would you do?
   a. I would shout or cry for help and alert my friend. ◯
   b. I would allow the stranger to steal the toys. ◯

Workout

Complete the sentences using words in the help box. Write the first letters of the answers in the box to make a new word.

1. She was dressed .... ☐
2. .... is the one sport that he is really good in. ☐
3. .... along, Jane. Don't be so slow . ☐
4. The lion had a reputation for being .... ☐
5. The .... pigeon asked the monkey to help him. ☐
6. A gold .... makes a wonderful pet. ☐

7. 'Don't touch them! They are .... documents'.

8. A .... is also known as the 'ship of the desert'.

9. The .... was scared of the mouse.

The new word is ....

Happiness Box

1. Make a 'Concern for Others' badge

You need

- A coloured pastel sheet
- Pencil
- Scissors
- Glue
- Star stickers
- Safety pin
- 2 ribbons

Steps

1. Draw the shape for your badge on the pastel sheet.
2. Cut out the shape.
3. Write 'Concern for Others' on it.
4. Decorate the shape as you like.
5. Make a bow using the ribbons and stick it to the badge.
6. Wear the badge on your shirt.

2. Read about J.L. Kaul, a blind social worker. Write a short paragraph on how you think his works have influenced the life of others.

Teaching tips

- Stress on the fact that universal love and concern makes the world a better place to live in.
- When people care for each other, they love and protect each other.
- Tell the class about the different social reformers and activists in India.

11. Walk Alone

Discuss

Look at the pictures. Talk about them in class.

Read along

Given below is an English translation of the Bengali poem *Akelo Chalo Re* by Rabindranath Tagore.

Walk Alone

Walk alone,
If they answer not to your call, walk alone,
If they are afraid and cower[1] mutely[2] facing the wall,
O thou unlucky one,
Open your mind and speak out alone.

If they turn away, and desert[3] you when crossing the wilderness[4],
O thou unlucky one,
Trample[5] the thorns under thy tread[6],
And along the blood-lined track travel alone.

If they shut doors and do not hold up the light when the night is troubled with storm,
O thou unlucky one,
With the thunder flame of pain ignite[7] your own heart,
And let it burn alone.

1. to crouch down in fear;
2. without saying anything;
3. to leave;
4. an uncultivated and inhospitable region in which nobody can live;
5. to step on with the purpose of destroying;
6. to walk in a particular manner;
7. cause to catch fire

Remember

- Respect all your national symbols.
- Learn the national anthem.
- Do your work properly and loyally.
- Respect the defence forces who protect your country.
- Protect national property.

Figure out

Write in your own words what you have understood from the poem.

....

....

....

....

....

....

....

....

....

....

....

Relate

Draw a 🙂 for the best answer.

1. If somebody is not showing respect to your national flag, what would you do?

   a. I would try to explain to him how he is disrespecting his country. ◯

   b. I would watch silently. ◯

2. In what way can you be a patriot?
   a. By being a good citizen and obeying rules. ◯
   b. By spoiling national monuments. ◯

3. On Republic Day, what would you do?
   a. I would enjoy the holiday and wake up late. ◯
   b. I would wake up early to watch the magnificent parade. ◯

Workout

1. Paste a picture of each theme. Also, write a few lines about each.

Tourist spots of India	Rivers of India	States of India
Mountains of India	Dances of India	Foods of India
Lakes of India	Monuments of India	Museums of India

2. You must have seen the Indian tricolour. Find out what each colour in the flag and the Ashoka Chakra stand for.

Saffron colour : ....

White colour : ....

Green colour : ....

Blue colour : ....

Ashoka Chakra : ....

Happiness Box

1. **Make a tricolour flag pin**

You need

- Paper
- Ruler
- Colours
- Tape
- Pencil
- Scissors
- Safety pin

Steps

1. From a sheet of stiff paper, cut out a rectangle
2. Draw the tricolour on the rectangle.
3. Colour the Ashoka Chakra on the tricolour.
4. Tape the safety pin to the back of the tricolour.
5. Stick flag pin is ready.

Your friends and you can wear this tricolour flag pin to show how much you love your country.

2. **Look at any Indian currency note. The denomination of the note is written on it in different languages. Count how many languages are used. Also, find out and write the names of these languages.**

Teaching tips

- Move beyond the regular icons shown in the Indian freedom movement in history, and tell students about lesser known people.
- Tell students of how there were some British who actually helped Indians to free the country from many evils.
- Encourage the students to share the ways in which they can be patriots.

12. The Loyal Mongoose

Initiative

Discuss

Look at the pictures. Talk about them in class.

Read along

Once upon a time, there lived a poor priest with his wife in a small village. The priest used to perform *pujas* at religious functions that took place in the villages nearby. They were a happy couple, but they had no children. After offering many prayers for a child, at last, a son was born to them.

The priest's wife had a mongoose as her pet. The mongoose was very loyal. He used to guard the priest's house and also looked after the baby, while it slept in the cradle.

One day, some people came to invite the priest to perform a puja in their house. *Pandit ji,* if you could come and perform the puja just now, we would be obliged'.

Hearing this, the priest was puzzled. His wife had gone to fetch water from the well on the outskirts of the village. So there was nobody to mind the baby. 'Should I go to perform the puja or stay at home to look after my baby? What should I do, God?' thought the priest. Finally, he decided to make the mongoose sit near the baby and go for the puja. 'Wife will come home in a short while. The baby will be safe, I am sure!' Thinking this, the priest left to perform the puja.

The mongoose sat beside the cradle guarding the baby as he always did. Suddenly, he saw a big, black snake slithering towards the cradle. Snakes are natural enemies

of mongooses. To protect the baby, he pounced upon the snake. After a fierce fight, the snake gave up. It realized that the mongoose would never let him hurt the baby. During the fight, the mongoose had been bitten by the snake. But, he ignored his own wounds. The mongoose was simply happy that he had done his duty faithfully and saved the baby from the snake.

Satisfied that the baby was now safe, the mongoose went to sleep beside him. Soon the priest's wife came back. As she walked in to check on her baby, she was surprised to see that the mongoose was badly hurt. She then checked the baby carefully. Satisfied that the baby was safe, she bandaged the mongoose. She knew in her heart that the mongoose had somehow saved her child.

Think and Say

Your pet dog is barking continuously. Will you shout at him to keep quiet or would you get up to see why is he barking?

Remember

- Loyalty is being faithful to people, country or ideas.
- Be supportive of the people who are loyal to you.
- Don't talk behind anybody's back.

Figure out

A. Tick (✓) the correct answers.

1. The priest used to perform pujas in religious functions taking place
   a. in the nearby villages. ☐
   b. in the nearby towns. ☐

2. The priest did not know what to do as
   a. the wife was not at home.
   b. the mongoose was not at home.
3. The mongoose sat beside
   a. the bed guarding the old man as he always did.
   b. the cradle guarding the baby as he always did.
4. The snake gave up because
   a. it realized that the mongoose would never give up and would not let it harm the baby.
   b. it saw another baby.
5. The mongoose did not care that he was hurt because
   a. he was loyal to the family and wanted to protect the baby.
   b. he did not feel any pain.

B. Answer these questions orally.

1. When the priest had to leave home, where was his wife?
2. Why did the mongoose attack the snake?
3. Why did the priest's wife think that the mongoose had saved her baby in some way or the other?

Relate

Draw a ☺ for the best answer.

1. If you see your pet cat sitting near a bowl of spilt milk in the kitchen, what would you do?
   a. I would hit it and shout at it.
   b. I would try to find out what had actually happened.
2. If you see your younger brother lying to a friend in the park, what would you do?
   a. I would do nothing.
   b. I would tell my brother later that he did a wrong thing.

3. Your friend is sick and has not been coming to school. What can you do?
   a. I can go to my friend's place, sit with him and make him feel better.
   b. I can go out to play and not bother about my friend. He will come to school when he recovers.

Workout

Complete this acrostic for RESPECT.

Relationship: I value our relationship.

E ....

S ....

P ....

E ....

C ....

T ....

Happiness Box

1. Dogs are known to be very loyal animals. Let's make a paper dog.

You need

- A square piece of white or coloured paper
- Black sketch pen

Steps

1.

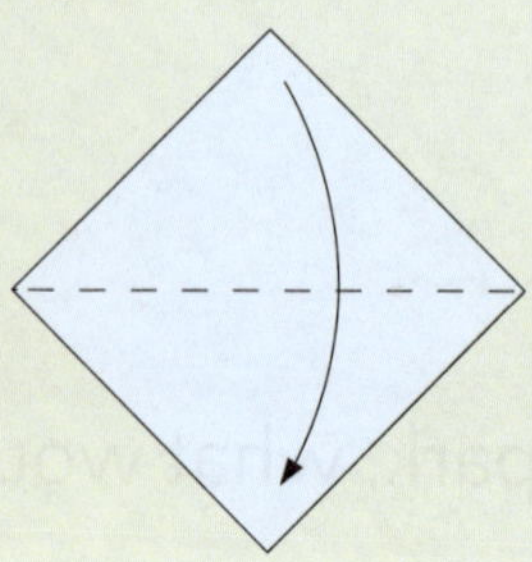

Fold the square piece of paper in half diagonally.

2.

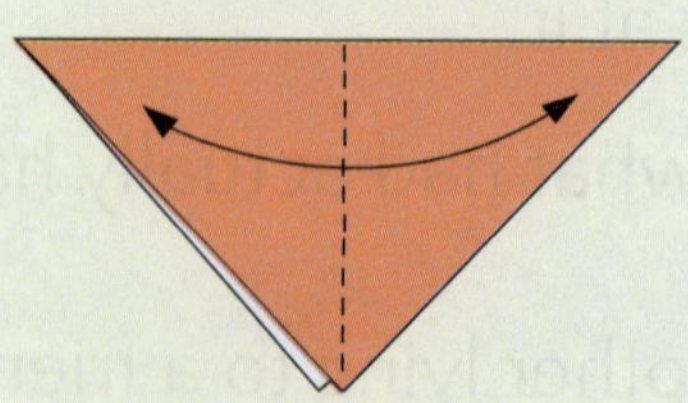

Fold again and open to make a centre crease.

3.

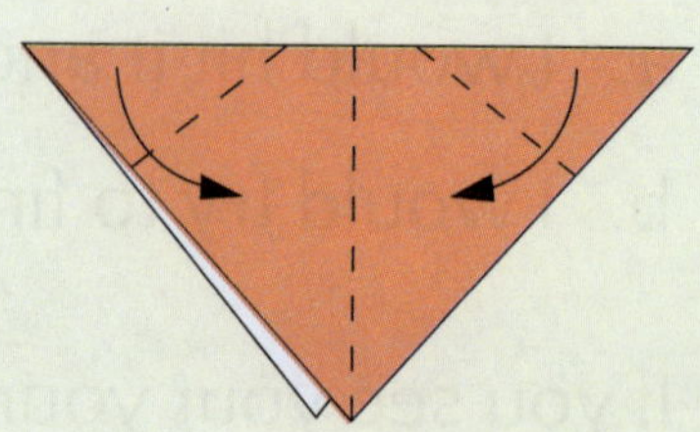

Fold the corners as shown to make the ears.

4.

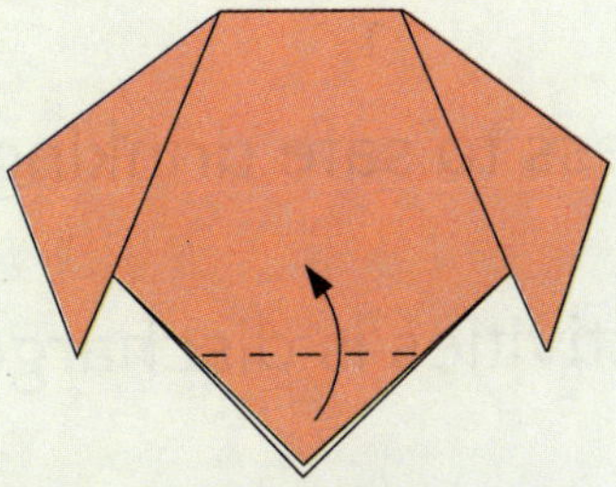

Fold on the dotted line.

5.

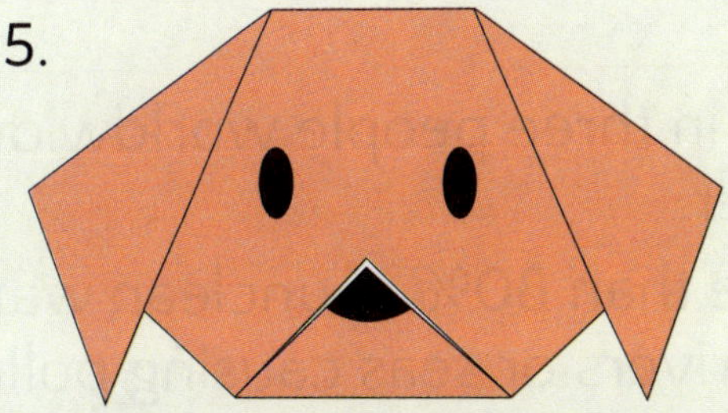

Draw the eyes and the nose on the dog's face.

2. Complete the word ladder using the last letter of each of the given words.

Teaching tips

- Focus on how the mongoose would not have given up even if it was overpowered.
- Tell students that loyalty comes from within and can be shown in a multitude of ways.
- Explain that loyalty does not mean allowing your loved ones to do wrong things.

Goal 6: Clean Water and Sanitation

- One in three people worldwide do not have access to safe drinking water.
- More than 80% of unclean water from human activities is discharged into rivers or seas causing pollution.
- Thousands of people do not have a basic hand washing facility .

Save Water!

Close running taps and leaking pipes in the house.

Many people do not get water in their home and have to go far to collect it.

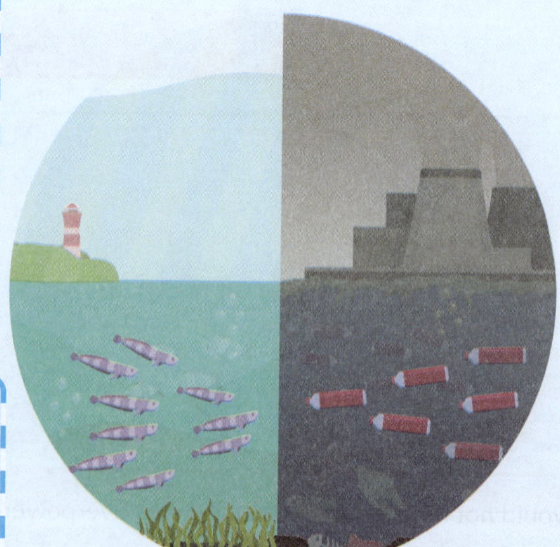

Use waste kitchen water for watering plants.

Do not throw waste and plastic into water bodies.

Take A Stand!

- About 3 billion people globally lack access to basic sanitation.
- Hundreds of children die every day from diseases caused by poor hygiene.
- The COVID-19 pandemic has demonstrated the importance of sanitation and hygiene for preventing and containing diseases.

Don't touch your nose, mouth or eyes with dirty hands. Use a handkerchief while coughing and sneezing.

During the COVID-19 pandemic, hand hygiene can save lives. Wash hands and stay clean!

Maintain a proper cleanliness routine daily to fight germs!

Use a mask when stepping out during the pandemic.

Project II : Building Character Strength

There are two types of mindsets: Flexible Mindsets and Flat Mindsets.

Flexible Mindsets: People belonging to flexible mindsets use sentences like:

- Let me try it.
- I can do it.
- Let me see, if it is interesting.

Flat Mindsets: People belonging to these mindsets often use sentences like:

- I can't do it.
- It's of no use.
- I am not interested.

Your personality may also have features of both these types of mindsets. Identify the different areas like trying out new dresses, changing team members, and interacting with people of different cultures, where you have a particular kind of a mindset and fill in the grid.

Flexible Mindset	Flat Mindset